THE 53RD STATE OCCASIONAL NO. 2

edited by Will Arbery

53SP 28
December 2018
Brooklyn, NY

53rdstatepress.org

The 53rd State Occasional No. 2
© 53rd State Press 2018

ISBN no. 978-9897393-7-5

Printed in the United States of America

THE 53RD STATE OCCASIONAL NO. 2

edited by Will Arbery
December 2018
53rd State Press
Brooklyn, NY

ALEX BORINSKY
MATTY DAVIS
MASHUQ MUSHTAQ DEEN
CORINNE DONLY
DAVID GREENSPAN
PHILLIP HOWZE
JULIA JARCHO
MODESTO FLAKO JIMENEZ
MIA KATIGBAK
MJ KAUFMAN
KRISTINE HARUNA LEE
SOFYA LEVITSKY-WEITZ
DAAIMAH MUBASHSHIR
RACHEL MARLENE KAUDER NALEBUFF
CAITLIN RYAN O'CONNELL
ZACH RUFA
REN DARA SANTIAGO
CELINE SONG
JORDAN TANNAHILL
KATE TARKER
ALICE TUAN
KORDE ARRINGTON TUTTLE
& MADELINE WISE

Each edition of the Occasional invites a guest editor to talk with artists, thinkers, and members of our community about questions we have and topics that move us.

In this second issue, Will Arbery asks:

something about an invitation . . .

I'm curious about invitations, and yeah I invite you to be curious about invitations too. I want to know who is invited to your show. Or what that invitation looks like. Or what an invitation is to you. Or if there is more that you're inviting than people. Is there an event, a collision, an upheaval, a nesting doll of more invitations, a silence you're inviting?

What –
where –
when –
who –
why –
how do you invite?

Is pandemonium invited?

(Of course I invite you to ignore all of these questions and just respond to: *something about an invitation* . . .)

But now I'm interested in where you draw the line. Where does the invitation stop? Where does the show become yours and yours alone? Is there a wall? (How do you feel about walls?) And then if there's a wall, is there an open part of that wall? (Or if it's all openness, is there a closedness somewhere in that openness?)

Because I'm curious to know who you *don't* invite to your show.

I make shows that are love letters to my family, and then I don't invite them.

I get really lonely back there in my chair. Watching my show back there, I'm just a wart. Then I see that I put a hole in my show, where my collaborators climbed in and built their own invitations and now, look, they're sending them out. How did that happen, it's so nice. And then I see the audience crawling towards the stage, giggling in the dark, I can't believe it. And when I leave the theater, my mom has texted me in all caps, something about this holy day of obligation, and did I honor it.

ALEXANDER BORINSKY

Something about an invitation . . .

1.

I invite all the people I want to prove wrong. I
write out of anger and disgust.
Ideas are bullshit. Boy-genius, with your formula-
tion of the week, go home.
Come back when what you have to say stinks of
onion and cum.
None of you know how filthy I can be, how I'd
bend over for you.

"I THINK THAT A POEM SHOULD BE THE
WORK OF A [GAL] WHO REALLY MEANS TO
DRIVE A NAIL" (George Oppen).

2.

We live in a time of lameness and hypocrisy, and
there's no outside to flee to (Timothy Morton).
Each of us is powerless to stop the pillage of life.

I desire that my texts sometimes limp, that they not
fold properly. ("The trunk of the play wouldn't

close . . . we had to hold it shut with a bungee and it was bouncing the whole drive to the theater.")

Fantasies of beauty, efficiency, and formal perfection are unseeing and a dead weight to us at this point in history.

There's no such thing as being smarter than anyone else, there's just honoring the particularity of your perception.

3.

I have to reckon with the world and take it up. A performer has to reckon with a text and take it up.

Pick your text carefully, but then:

Keep faithful to the text as-written. When you memorize verbatim your mind stretches outside of itself towards words that don't curve the way your inclinations curve. I demand that you reach outside of yourself even to this small and ungainly preposition. I put it there, yes, on purpose.

I invite you to reckon with something that can't quite be assimilated.
The project is to see *what is,* and acknowledge it, because it is stranger than what we think we see. The project is not to see *what is close to what we recognize,* nor *what we hoped for.*

Texts have particular histories. Texts have ancestors. So do each of us. So do all of us, together.

4.

I write out of anger and disgust, yes, and end up making sweet and melancholy work. (Sigh.)

I have been reading the Psalms lately. The Psalms are a project in language I have a lot of time for. They aren't perfect, but that's part of why they interest me. They are prickly, with the palm-rubbed-under-belly-feel of liturgy.

Liturgy is often ill-fitting. It cannot quite be assimilated and tugs us out of ourselves.
Liturgy invites us into a language-room we can occupy together, if temporarily.

Insofar as it is baggy it can accommodate private
and idiosyncratic experience.
(I am not relenting when I say there is no smart,
there is only attention to how one perceives.)

We need ill-fitting language to reckon with *what is*.
What is has history. *What is* brings in the ancestors.
Baggy, prickly language ducks the ahistorical lie
of formal perfection. Of dramaturgy as "let's fix
this thing."

(To said dramaturg, I reply: Fuck you. What are
you risking? What of yourself are you putting on
the line?)

What follows liturgy is coffee, tea, maybe a meal.
Wandering around the fellowship hall and chatting
with all the people. I do like that part, it's true.

I like singing with people. I like rooms big enough
for all of us, prickly and distinct.

5.

Who am I kidding.
I want to drive you all away, and then I find myself

in a room with you, sweet enough to come. Laughing like it's always what I intended.

I am still in search of strong verbs for our powerless age.
I am still not interested, boy-genius, in your ideas and universals.

I don't want freedom. I want meaningful relation.

MATTY DAVIS

Invitations significantly contribute to the 15 GB fullness of my inbox. (These are invitations that I have sent.) I love and become obsessed. A bit intuitive, off-the-cuff, and without a well organized email list, I sometimes systematically push each key of the keyboard, seeing what names might be evoked, searching for anyone whom I might have missed and hope to see.

Invitations half break my heart, confound me, burn bridges in my mind—bridges that maybe didn't exist in the first place. I once invited someone I personally met and shared mutual enjoyment with to every performance I did for five years. They never came. They never said why. I still want them to be there! I still invite them.

Sometimes I find myself inviting the wrong people. These invitations hurt, both before and after. They're this vacuous longing. They're the kind of invitation that you send to the kind of person in whom you maybe have this really fucked up belief that if they see your show they'll set you free.

I try to focus on inviting people who might be connected to a work's content, but who might not give much of a shit about art. Like my grandfather who worked in the steel mills—he understands hammers, metal, and work. Like the arborist at the Field Museum—she knows how long into autumn a mulberry tree holds its leaves. Like a runner, who sensually knows distance. It feels like unique transformation is possible there, like there might be a bridge.

(I realize that I don't invite enough friends to my house. I realize I am never invited to my friends' houses anymore. No one says, "Wanna come over?")

Sometimes making work is a more interesting kind of invitation. Just last week I invited snakes, ticks, and poison ivy. We accessed a former clandestine airstrip in remote Arkansas . . . My arms are oozing puss. My girlfriend has little pimples on her legs where ticks lodged their heads and legs. A guy named Chris recently washed the scales of a cottonmouth off his machete. We invited it all, but the snake didn't invite the slash.

MASHUQ MUSHTAQ DEEN

I *do not invite* rustling in your seats. Or unwrapping candies. I do not invite getting up to pee during the show. It's pretty rigid of me, I know, but it's just so fucking hard to perform this 85-minute show by myself. And they said—everyone said—it would get easier. And it never got easier. Not after a week in NC. Not after a month in DC. Definitely not after that month in NYC.

(That last one almost broke me.)

This show is definitely an invitation. To all. (Not just to my community, but to *all*.) And I'm a stickler about that. My job: do what the title says: *Draw the Circle*. Be sneaky. Don't let the audience in on the game. Without you even knowing it, I was going to put you inside my heart. And maybe— *maybe*—you would put me inside yours. And there was another invitation: to draw your own circles, to put other people inside your heart, to see your heart as a vast place—

But then.

(Did I mention that the NYC show almost broke me?)

Because the past came streaming through the performance, through the fifth wall that no one talks about, and into the present. Some howling, angry, scared, fearful beast came clawing hisher way back to the present. And was that because I *had* invited himher, or because I *hadn't* invited himher? . . . Or was it just the memory of things that used to be?

Thirty minutes before curtain on a Friday, I sat on the stage and cried. Snot ran down my face. Because I was breaking. And I wouldn't say this was a positive experience. But it is ironic, because in my work, the invitation is to break apart. A hardened heart cannot grow bigger. But all breaking comes with risk, I suppose.

I think that I will always take the bigger risk, the more dangerous one. I think that's my job, so that you will trust me enough to allow yourself to be broken. But that's also naïve, because who can ever truly know another's breaking?

CORINNE DONLY

These days, I think most about reading. Reading is what I mostly do. There are occasional upwellings of sentence within me, but, lonely creatures!, they are lines without community. There is no larger project—not even a larger paragraph—in mind.

Still, much has been made of the fragment. Or of the effort to make sense of a world learned in pieces. My students and I recently read *Don't Let Me Be Lonely* together, and so I have Claudia Rankine's words for guidance:

> *Sometimes you read something and a thought that was floating around in your veins organizes itself into the sentence that reflects it.*

I am drawn to this quote not only because it enacts in me the very thing it describes—nudging me into naming my own experience as a writer—but also because it hints at a mystery I perceive in the interactions of certain texts with their readers. This is a mystery about the connection between the generous and the generative—about how and when and why one person's language can invite another's into existence.

~

I keep a notebook open on my dresser, as usually I want to write just as I am hurriedly putting on clothes, already late to wherever I'm headed. One morning, I had been reading an essay by Bonnie Marranca on Gertrude Stein's landscape theatre. I was feeling grateful to Stein, as I feel grateful to Rankine, for how her uses of language have shifted my habits of seeing. And so I wrote this:

> *Every time I read Stein, I rejoice in the invitation: If you take me seriously, I will unsettle you.*

When I first sat down to compose this essay, I returned to my notebook for inspiration. Spotting the above sentence—with the word "invitation" right at the center of it—I conceived of an essay about the many invitations that I receive from Stein. The piece was to be about the impossibility of affixing definitive meanings to Stein's texts and about why that impossibility makes me feel welcome as her reader—as if the texts need me, in all my perspectival particularity, to complete them. I imagined an essay, in other words, about those joyful literary moments when interpretation becomes synonymous with invitation.

But then, my sentence did not grow. I carried it around with me for weeks, muttering it under my breath as I searched for the words that came next. I was trying to discover the *thought floating around in my veins* (as Rankine would say)— the one waiting to be *organized* as a response. I repeated and repeated my own initial fragment until, at some point, I noticed: more than the content of Stein's writing, I was concerned with the shift—with the productive undoing of comfort— that Stein's syntaxes can accomplish within me. By choosing to celebrate Stein, I was, in fact, asking myself to acknowledge: I feel most respected by a text whenever I am challenged by it; I feel most welcomed within interpretive spaces that both ask me to show up exactly as I am *and* return me to the world inhabiting it less easily.

~

As a white person, I recognize how important it is that I be invested—artistically, interpersonally, and in an ongoing way—in the conditions of my own *unsettling*. And as I seek to understand, on deeper and deeper levels, what this unsettling looks like within me, it is probably only fitting that I find my writing arriving in fragments—that my sentences are calling for long periods of investigation before they are ready to grow into something more.

Perhaps that's why I feel so pulled to read—ever eager to spend time with writers whose very acts of language complicate my easy explanations of the world and, consequently, invite me into new language. In allowing me to carry their sentences within me—to repeat and repeat fragments from their larger works—these writers teach me how very generous an incompleteness can be. They hold the door open, prompting me (even now) to rearticulate myself.

Inviting me to see the fragment as a more sincere call for conversation and community, not an indication of their absence.

DAVID GREENSPAN

I encourage friends and colleagues to attend a play I'm performing in when I think the play or my performing in the play will be of especial interest to them and that the play and part are particularly important to me. Otherwise, I let a few close friends and colleagues know in the course of everyday interaction.

If it's a play of mine—and typically I'm performing in it—and it's thus particularly important to me I let everyone I know know and let them know I sincerely hope they will have an opportunity to attend. If it's a performing project that I've initiated and is thus particularly important to me I do likewise.

If I really want someone to attend for personal or professional reasons I invite them: I offer to make arrangements—either complimentary tickets or tickets I purchase. There are always a few friends and colleagues whose finances I know make theatergoing prohibitive and I know they like to go to the theater so whenever possible I offer them comps. There are professional relationships I want to maintain or foster and so when I ask someone like that to attend it is always with the understanding that I will make arrangements. Though funny enough on many occasions the person or persons I've invited insist on paying and I like to do likewise when I'm in that position.

I don't invite my family because they're either dead or far away. And when it comes to my plays if they knew what I was saying about them they'd plotz. An aunt of mine once attended a play of mine that was about her and that I had not invited her to see and I think she was perfectly happy about it because she didn't understand it.

If the play is now a show it is something shared. If you're asking people to see it it's because you want to share it—you're willing to show it. If somebody sees it it's because you're showing it, you're willing to have it seen—and of course people see what you're showing, they hear the lines you've written. That's also true when someone reads the play, they hear and see but they don't hear and see as they would hear and see if they attended a performance. Either way the play becomes their experience as well as your experience.

I rarely watch my plays because I'm usually performing in them. Sometimes I'm invited to see a play of mine out-of-town—and I'm nervous watching it because they're not doing it as I did it and I can see things that are wrong about the play or lacking in the play that I didn't see when I was performing in it—or they're not doing it correctly.

But I really can't think of anything interesting to say about invitations and don't think I've done so. But now I'll tell you an interesting story—or a story that is interesting to me.

~

Not so long ago I attended a Sunday service and during the prayers of the people an elderly black man stood in the aisle and spoke loudly, appealing for help—food or money it seemed, though I could not fully understand his words. I regularly attend Sunday service and I had noticed this man earlier in the service because I had not noticed him before—and it's a largely white congregation.

A young, recently ordained priest is a member of our clergy—our curate, Father Bo. Young as he is, he always delivers engaging, intelligent sermons—and I have a good feeling about him. Our rector was absent—as I believe was the senior associate priest—that Sunday when the man asked for help. Father Bo stepped down from his seat on the dais, approached the man and spoke quietly with him for a moment or two. Well it was very interesting because he did not escort him up the aisle and out of the church, he ushered him further into the church to speak further with him—for the man was clearly distressed. After a while Father Bo returned to his seat and the man returned to the pew with a package where he remained throughout the rest of the service. Afterwards, Father Bo and several parishioners spoke further with him. I have not seen that man since—that elderly man who was very nicely dressed in a suit and tie—but I thought of that incident when asked to reflect on invitation.

PHILLIP HOWZE

conjecture

It needs to be more accessible

                              I'm sorry?

More people need to access it

                              More people—

—need access
Generally speaking. In general.
The general population.
How are you helping them, you
know?

                    Is that what I should be doing?

Not specifically, but generally.
A helping hand is always better than
a biting one.

                                        But.
                        Hands don't bite.

I mean.

I think I was thinking about that
saying. On biting the hand.

———

You know?

———

Don't bite the hand that feeds you.
That's.

I don't understand what that has to
do with—

This isn't—I'm not really talking about
us, about people like you and me.
I'm talking about other people.
You have to make it clear and intentional for people.

You think it's not intentional?

It is and it isn't.

———

You understand?

                    I don't understand.
                      Is it, or isn't it?

It's just not very specific.
Not specific enough in the ways that
people are used to. You know?
It's not broadly specific.

———

There should be something about it
that's more specific in general.
A thing that reminds people, generally, of something specific. Like.
Like: Martin Luther King, Jr.

———

Okay that's a bad example. But you
know what I mean.

———

                    You're saying it should be more like
                          a bad example.

No God no.
I'd never say that to you. NO.

You. Do. You.

———

But also maybe you could try to do
it like other people do.
You know?

No.

It's just.
I can see myself having to do a lot of
explaining on your behalf.

———-

———-

Or not.
You could not do that, and just let
people ponder it.

Yes, but no. I can't really do that.

They're smart. They'll figure
something out, won't they?

———

———

No.

                                   No?

Yes.
Yes, no.

                                   O.

———

                                ———-

———-

                   Are you sure about that?

JULIA JARCHO

It was a really long time before I had any romance in my life. I mean with another person. I did read plenty of teen magazines and books that featured romance pretty heavily. I liked sad endings best; I would cry for hours. I could go on for a while about *West Side Story* with its characters as dubiously puerto rican as me—did you know they published the screenplay in a paperback together with *Romeo and Juliet*? I brought it to sleepaway camp and read it at night with a flashlight and daddylonglegses crawling all over my bunk—anyway it was the eighties and then the nineties and for me there was no kissing but there was—*so* there was—this great unpeopled desire, which opened out in the presence of whatever landscapes were hints of a very other way of being. Industrial districts, vacant lots, the railing by the river, anyplace empty.

Who was I going to find there? Eventually someone else would have to show up, I guess. But I really didn't have any idea of who it could be. I liked Robert Sean Leonard or unfortunately Christian Bale, but even if one of them turned up there it would've been all wrong. It wasn't anyone with a body and it for sure wasn't my body. It was a possibility of being transformed and lost. With my plays I am always trying to find my way back to that dingy white street where desire can shed its skin and stop having to answer for itself.

So when you ask me who it's for—who's invited— this is what I think of. First I think: well, anyone who can see me, save me from feeling like I don't exist. Then I think: no, it's that other thing, the excitement of *not* existing, just waiting to burst in and blow me back to that empty place if we can get the right combo of rhythms and stumbles and laughs. I have to hide out in the dressing room before the show. I'm a disaster, I can't look at you: I'm humiliated that you caught me wanting something so much.

MODESTO FLAKO JIMENEZ

Pt.1 Invitation: Arcoíris De Dreamers

We invite you. Seriously
Simple request . . . entra.
Nuestras puertas están abiertas.
You haven't killed our humanity
We can still breathe
Even con tu presión en el cocote.

Watering those cracks en tu Arcoíris
We must pass by space, water & time
To really see our beauty from slavery,
Dictatorship y deportación
We stay Oprah-dreaming
Hi Celie.

Bienvenido to our rainbow
Nature's greatest accomplishment
All the colors debajo del sol
Where the turtle wins
Without hurting the rabbit
Making birds chirp summer shine

Mira nuestro Arcoíris de Dreamers

Everything must not be a debate
A political statement
A stand
To your cracker barrel ass
Can I breathe?

We must all see nuestro Arcoíris
That self-invitation to clarity
Esa Alegría con nuestro inner azúcar salsera,
Ese amor furioso,
Dale kindness, a tu inclusiveness
Y llena lo de compasión

Te invito to your Arcoíris sin colores
We know it's hard to face
Imagínate abrazar your unknown?
You must stare at your true colors
From the Red Tara plantation soil
To those Yankee Blues.

Where are you really from americano?
Tell us about your history
Blanco is not a place.
Do the fucking work!
Nike that shit and Just Do It!
Mama Mercedes y Ahmed go through it.

Mi gente miren bien a los Arcoíris
Que ellos invitan que gatan lentamente
Antes de aceptar su mic check, mic check
Check su dance, check su Dribble
Check su lanzar
Cuidado with them fuku contracts

Stop inviting us to your Arcoíris teatral
To our past tétrica trauma
Stop asking POC for certain colors
It's our choice to write about it
Esos momentos esperpentos
Eternally embedded on loop

Nuestra vida, un baile sin parada
Do the FUCKING work blankitos
400 years haven't taught you
That you can't break our spirit
Este melanin es Magia bacana
Afro-latina, caribeña americana

Is that why we get those Grants Arcoíris?

Staring at your rainbow sin color
Constantly visiting our trauma
For your pleasure

Within our sanctuary spaces
Esos pisos negros
Llenos de colores que pintamos

To put pomade on bruises
Then SHINE in front of you
then wash it out in the dressing room
Remember 'Every nigga is a star'
Ya love shooting down
Slowly nowadays

I invite you mi gente Arcoíris
To not forget that every check
Is part of your melanin being sold
Helping them stay rich
Stay woke
In their seasonal plush seats

You invite me to disrespect the Arcoiris
Myself,
You,
Our humanity
Constantly for a check
Those days are done locón!

How does a futuro get imagine Arcoíris?

If we don't start to detallarlo ourselves
Comenzar a pintar el canvas
Planting positive blossoming light
Painting those blocks llenos de brilliance
Start small don't rush

Remember refraction has happened Arcoíris
The white light has scattered through it all
Deseado y no deseado, ha tocado todo
It has not seen us without force
Tienes que bailar en esas aguas
Y simply accept

Entonces sigue pintando ese Arcoíris
With more positive images of oneself
That beautiful vision of what we are
Where we could all be headed
Pero todos debemos pasar por el rainstorm
And your lapel is looking mighty dry my g!

We must flourish blossom out Arcoíris
This constant drought.
Let us never forget the cacti
Stores aqua. Ya sabe…
It has evolved pass the desert.
Sin cambiar su paisaje.

Drink échale agua a tus roots Arcoíris.
Nunca olvides tu proceso
No te pierdas en el constante
Querido Arcoíris semillita.
A beautiful vision
To come up with such magic

Know that the best time to see the Arcoíris
Is always going to be after the rainstorm
Has ended
Droplets y sunlight
Are needed for the Arcoíris
For the spectacle to happen.

Pt.2 Invitation: How to Make a Nuevo Arcoiris

(Start. Comienzo.)

1.
2.
3.
4.
5.
6.

1.
2.
3.
4.
5.
6.

1.
2.
3.
4.
5.
6.

1.
2.
3.
4.
5.
6.

1.
2.
3.
4.
5.

6.

1.
2.
3.
4.
5.
6.

1.
2.
3.
4.
5.
6.

by Gera Luz

MIA KATIGBAK

An Invitation

What does "intimate" mean? A few months ago, I wanted to invite just a few people to something I didn't even know what to call. But I wanted it to be special, something that showed my appreciation for how the guests were supporting the work that NAATCO, my company, does.

I am allergic to big grand things that make me feel like I'm patting myself on the back, or boasting, or misrepresenting myself. I do like hosting friends, though, and making people feel welcome. I like to have guests feel like they're in good company and that they can enjoy themselves whether they just want to sit quietly or socialize extensively.

I like an intimate group of people.

We ended up with forty-seven guests. Relatively speaking, I suppose that is an intimate group. That's about half an Off-Off-Broadway house, and we'd consider that a small house. We held the event in what was tantamount to an attic in the corner of an

Episcopalian church, a room that somewhat resembled a Victorian parlor that, though well maintained, had seen better days. We put candles and flowers all over, threw crisp white tablecloths on tables, and staged a model of our set dramatically in one corner. A member of my board walked in and said, "It's so NAATCO." I didn't quite know how to take that.

But then I thought, "Well, that's me." Nothing fancy, but generous amounts of good food and good wine, a pretty setting, and since we simulated the first day of rehearsals, the context and centerpiece was our work.

And I was able to talk to every single person in the room.

As NAATCO continues to grow, I will need to host more and bigger events. I suspect I will always be allergic, but I will be able to extend a gracious invitation if I bring what is most important to me as host to the proceedings. This goes for all the work we want to share with the world. With whom I can be intimate, as long as I willingly and happily share my pride and sensibility.

MJ KAUFMAN

What – A trans love story.
Where – A village on the edge of the sea in danger of being washed away.
When – The year of the sacrifice. The year astrologers predicted the world would be consumed by floods and fires, diseases and riots.
Who – Two boys dressed as girls dressed as boys.
Why – Because maybe queer love could avert disaster.

What – A support group for things inside of things.
Where – Basement of the church.
When – A dry, warm winter in Manhattan.
Who – A walrus in the body of a crocodile.
Why – You are more complex than you believe.

What – A sexual assault reckoning.
Where – A small liberal arts college.
When – Spring semester when the cherry blossoms are in bloom.
Who – Five women and nonbinary people.
Why – We live in a rape culture.

What – A kiss, a funeral, a Thanksgiving dinner.

Where – A forest of Ponderosa pines
When – Sagittarius time.
Who – A trans boy, his family, and the nature conservancy intern.
Why – Because every goodbye contains a hello? Because it pleases me.

What – An investigation of toxic masculinity.
Where – A working class living room, a queer cooperative house, a DIY bike collective, a loft belonging to a sweet older man.
When – Super Bowl Sunday.
Who – Men who like football and men who hate footfall. Men who have a lot to prove and men who have nothing to prove. Men who cry and work out and sell bikes and make love and cook dinner for their families and piss off their friends, but then realize it and apologize. Men who can change what being a man means.
Why – There were no good men yet.

What – A textual experiment in narrative and death.
Where – The theater.
When – Ancient Greece, Transcendental New

England, Weimar Germany, 1940's New Orleans, my father's living room, 2004, 2011, 2013.
Who – Me and all the dead people I've ever known.
Why – To find out if control over death in narrative could translate to control over death in life. To find out if we can truly cure ourselves through belief.

~

These are invitations to each of my plays from the last year.

You're invited to sit quietly in uncomfortable chairs. You're invited to respond appropriately when the actors pause. You're invited to laugh and cry and exclaim oh! when a line strikes you as profound. You're invited to clap at the end and maybe stand, but be discerning, don't stand every time. You're invited to comment politely. Potentially hide your true feelings. Be political about what you say to whom.

In my mind I'd like to ask audiences to be rebellious: to laugh and cry at the wrong times, to shout things out, come and go, get up and leave, storm the stage, throw things, who knows . . . but I don't actually want that. During my last play in production, I sat at the back of the darkened house wishing the audience would laugh less. Their laughter was so boisterous we were losing the story.

Now I'm sitting at a desk overlooking the hills of Los Angeles. I can see the mountains and the Hollywood sign in one direction and almost the ocean in the other. The things I write here have almost no invitation. They just are. I'll never know how audiences are watching them. I'll never know when they're laughing or crying or shouting at the screen. Or, to be real, shutting off the thing cuz they aren't into it. The lack of real invitation is hard for me. The lack of give and take, of in-the-moment-feedback, the lack of that real thing, that thing that gets exchanged when you're in theater, that live charge of understanding. I suppose that's what I'm in it for. An invitation to exchange energy. Sometimes I've wondered why a play that was so funny last night was sad tonight, why a play that read so quickly and smoothly in Philadelphia was a slog in New York, why you can't ever count on anyone to land a moment. It's that uncontrollable science experiment, the mix of energy and light

that is theater. You're invited to add your flavor.
The show won't exist without you.

KRISTINE HARUNA LEE

"I feel like I'm not allowed to own anything in this space, like my wants and desires are not supposed to come first . . . so I feel lost."
– a white collaborator

A conscious invitation takes time to show us the boundaries of any given space or process. Boundaries are walls, yes. And we all have our own edifice, ever shifting as we choose to connect with others. Then let us use boundaries to clarify *how* we are going to relate with each other, how we will communicate our individual needs without shame (what a humane way to acknowledge our differences!). Let us choose to believe each other's boundaries and respect them. And let us make space for those who must decline the invitation, for those who must leave. A conscious invitation practices an empathic kind of transparency—the opening of a mouth, a sharing of truths.

There are also dangerous invitations. These invitations are wholly unaware of a simple terror. Caused by seemingly benign privileges and biases rendered invisible by the dangerous invitation, a bare studio room rented by Brooklyn Artist who just wants to "try some things out." A dangerous invitation believes in a dangerous illusion: *that we are all free in the same ways*—and so it enacts a violence by asking for more and more labor without considering the bodily cost—and this cost may differ greatly depending on each soul. A dangerous invitation behaves as if there are no boundaries whatsoever, because it relishes the belief that one's ownership is *infinite*, and anything is possible.

Invitations as Practice

I invite my ancestors into my practice and in so doing I invite the chronic illness of my intergenerational trauma and pain.

I invite white folx to racialize their experiences and their art, too (i.e., can you name your white perspective out loud, and invite others to view it in this way? Can you use white emojis?).

I invite you to name the tyrannies you swallow day by day and attempt to make your own, until you will sicken and die from them, still in silence (Audre Lorde).

I invite you to consider whether you *need* to participate in order for it to *count*. (An invitation doesn't mean you have to speak first, nor does it mean your participation is a given.)

I invite you to decolonize your mind.

SOFYA LEVITSKY-WEITZ

Inside a play I once wrote:

I am evil and I invite evil.

Aristotle said something like:

Women have more pores to let the devil in.

Now, I think:

These are accurate descriptions of my plays. I want you inside them, trapped in there.

I want to get inside your brain, rip you inside out, leave you stammering.

Someone told me once:

There's the you I'm talking to now . . . and there's the you that writes your plays.

I'm scared of her, sometimes.

She's wild, she wants to blow things up.

Today, my mother talked about her.

That Sofya is a <u>survivalist</u>.

Is it women who have to split open in order to achieve something?

And when we achieve it, are we the ones who have to sacrifice everything else for it?

Who am I, when I invite it all in?

What am I left with, once it's gone?

And Faulkner said:

The only thing worth writing about is the heart in conflict with itself.

I used to say: writing plays feels like a possession. Like ghosts.

That feeling of rapid insanity you're experiencing could be the work of a dybbuk.

Rapid insanity. All at once.

When we invite the demon in, do we know what we're doing? Can we blame its cleverness, its careful words? Or did we lay out that welcome mat?

When we invited the demon in, were we lonely?
Did we like all those voices in our head with us?

When a play ends, it feels like a death. All those
character-people and all those real ones, all of us
in our séance together, summoning something.

I invite those voices, populating this space. I invite you
to see it, maybe. I try not to apologize ahead of time.

What is theatre, anyway, if not possession?

What is theatre, anyway, if not inviting in the
possibility of evil?

If I put you inside, I put myself in there first. I put
something raw and weird and I'm probably curling
up somewhere in the fetal position, humiliated.

But it's my pores that make me soft.

It's my sadness that makes me real.

It's my rage that makes me immortal.

I'm a vampire, invite me in.

Or: I'm already here, stay awhile.

DAAIMAH MUBASHSHIR

Come with Me (Solve for X)

Down this hill
Run with me
a force will pull at your legs
forward and down
the incline is steep

I want to tell you about where
I couldn't hear the singing
when I was restless
without agency
and discontent

Okay
Let's sit right here
See into the window

There is a bed
sheets tightly folded around
corners. Pillows Pillows
Pillows

next to it

a table where
a woman driven
makes something beautiful

Ah and that music is merely
sound from a speaker
which is not the
singing

Let's keep going
downward over the rocks
don't worry it's safe
I have your hand

Look into the dusk
towards the origin point

Do you see the figures bent over themselves
Hands touching something below

Do you see the reaching?

They're pulling your
puffy love
Piece by piece up from the ground

That rhythmic hum

is not the singing

It's there to mark
events that happened before
and after

All of which
are important

Shall we?

Let's go up the hill
on the other side

Careful of the thorns

Listen
No put your ear
up against this rock

What do you hear?

No it's not singing

That is crying

Close your eyes

See the girl

staring off into space

She just realized
her purpose
her truest raison d'être
is to benefit
you
and you alone

See she thought
she was going out
there day after day
to actualize
to finally get paid
to overcome the past
that origin
that point in time

You know
exactly what I mean

Now
she understands
that all that she created
will be consumed

a tasty treat for

a Saturday afternoon
for free

Wasn't she adorable to
go through all that trouble
to provide
for us

So Noble

Let's get out of here

Now we have to
run run run
across the bank
to the alcove

Turn left

Come with me
we are inside now

A shelter

I'll get the door for you

There is water on the counter
Help yourself

It's nice to just
take a breath
isn't it?

Great

Follow me down this hall

Here is a door

Before you enter
I want to ask you

No
wait
I want to invite you

Love the woman
sitting at the table
making something

beautiful

Offer her that drink
of water.

Take out your
wallet and pay her
for all the time she has
spent making you
warm and filled
with a love
you could never
replicate on your own

If you can
do that

I promise you

You will
hear the singing

Everytime I give her
my Love

Put money in her hands

For all the times

I've been held
and upheld
by what she made

I hear the singing:

contented breaths
undisputed power
a quiet mind

RACHEL MARLENE KAUDER NALEBUFF

I recently wrote an invitation that ended with a heart, and then removed several people from my email list. I thought the heart at the bottom would make them uncomfortable. It felt too intimate. And then I thought: why do I care so much? I would like to care less and to need less from what people do with my invitations.

While writing invitations, I am often tempted to explain why my work is urgent or important. Maybe I do this to convince myself that what I am doing is important. But this doesn't belong in an invitation. I do not want to convince you to come to my work. I want you to come if you want to come. But how to say this?

My most sincere invitation is an invitation to look at your own desire for how you want to spend your night. It might look a little something like this:

Dear friends,

Here is what is happening
Here is the date

On this date, how would you like to spend your time? This most precious commodity. I invite you to think about this. What brings you joy? What brings you down? What brings you sanity? Are you prepared to accept the unknowns and sacrifices that invariably accompany attendance?

Do you want to come? Do you really want to come? If you do not, you are not invited.

You are invited to your best evening. If your best evening includes this show, then you are invited.

<3

CAITLIN RYAN O'CONNELL

Invitation

verb
an intimate
devoted
gentle
bold
collision
of our senses
as we all sit in a dark room together

It feels like an alignment. Like bones cracking back into place, if only for a moment of relief, release. And then the aching starts again. Like the balm of green chilies and hemp seed oil warming your skin. Like a nerve pinching part of your body numb only to rediscover your limbs when the feeling comes back. It lacks stability and always has its own logic. Sometimes it's a plunge into chaos with little respite. Sometimes it's a leaning (hopefully in). Inviting the angle of voracious curiosity. It's a space attempting to listen without expectation. A space attempting silence that moves beyond anxiety. A space for obsession. For an unexpected fascination. Like the placement of her jaw. And with the obsession comes an endurance for alacrity beyond alacrity. It is a collision of limerence and lust and love that sets us off-balance from the comfort we once thought we needed. It lives in the dream of not needing to communicate everything to be understood. A momentary shorthand. Unexpected and fleeting, but it was there for a moment. It is full of feisty collaborators. Young and old. Full of naïve optimism and exceptional small wisdoms. Collaborators willing to move through the calamity, the muck, the overstimulation to find the place of ease. Like an alignment. Like bones cracking back into place, if only for a moment of relief, release. And then the aching starts again.

ZACH RUFA

I think of the invitation in my work as a mode of intervention. It's a disruption of the status quo of who is invited to the table. I am a disabled playwright who writes stories with disabled characters. I do this because it is how I have experienced the world my entire life, but also because it feels vitally important, and because I feel that it is my responsibility to my people to do so.

My disabled characters aren't symbols. Disability in my work is not an outward reflection of who a person is. It is not reflective of the deformed evil of Richard III, or the broken frailty of Laura playing with her glass menagerie. It is simply a thing that happens, sometimes.

I write my invitation in the language of my characters' bodies. I write it in the singular, inimitable forms we take. I think a lot of the time, people think that disability means that there is something less to a person, something missing. They think that I am missing a leg, or that someone who is deaf is missing their hearing. Because of this, I find that people often think that they can somehow 'lessen' themselves to inhabit a disabled role. That an able-bodied actor can sit in a chair and pretend to be paralyzed or can learn their lines in sign language and pretend that they can't hear lines being spoken to them.

I think that's bullshit.

We're not less, we are simply different. In that way, the invitation in my work also comes from who is not invited. It comes in the moments when my characters do what is impossible for able-bodied actors. The invitation comes in the form of things that are for us so simple. It's a character taking their leg off onstage and hopping around. It's in the things I can do that able-bodied people cannot do.

That said, I want my work to be for everyone. I want it to be an invitation for every kind of person, regardless of their ability, or any of the other things that make us remarkably distinct beings, to inhabit something together. I invite all our beautiful differences.

To be honest, I'm getting really tired of writing

disabled characters and then having to be the one to also play those parts, because we couldn't find another disabled actor.

And yet, I'm still going to keep on writing those parts.

My work is an open invitation.

REN DARA SANTIAGO

Dear Reader,

I was seventeen when I almost fucked the devil.

But I have been haunted since I was a kid. Nothing made sense to me. Few things felt real or honest.

It started with deadness tingling under my skin as I fought sleep paralysis. It made the silence incredibly loud. The buzz and whispers and panting and metal and electronics were magnified; every apartment on the block came into my room through sound— growing so loud it was white noise—flooding my ears and dropping me into an unknown version of where I might exist—until I heard one voice; or a collective evil. The first time I met a demon, it pulled the emptiness in my room into a dense shifting form that stopped time. It split my head open with cold nothing and a black hole opened in my mind. A black hole that I can't close. I can only keep my soul from falling into it.

The devil came to visit me like this great, Russian novel. I remember I was just sitting in my friend's room while she was out of town. I was looking out the window. And then I was looking behind me, the door was open behind me, and my friend walked in. And out the window it was cloudy, it was a heavy forecast morning, but inside, when I looked behind me, the room was filled with sunshine. Like, bright and natural, but cold, kinda. And my friend stood in the doorway like she wasn't out of town for the next two weeks and I wasn't alone. And she told me to put eggshells on the windowsill like they were directions to the grocery store. Eggshells on the window. When she said it, I saw it; two eggshells, in half. Like I cracked an egg, cleaned it out and dried it on the outside of the kitchen windowsill, the window that opened to a crucible of other windows in the apartment; when you looked up you got an oculus to the clouds and down below a well of trash that other people threw out their window. The vision freaked me out so I looked away from my friend, back out the window and when I looked behind me, she was gone. The room was filled with shadow and the door was closed. I was scared of what I felt in that vision, but I had to know what it meant. I cracked an egg, cleaned out the white shells, placed them as close to picture perfect in my head, and left the window open a crack. And that was how I invited him in.

He told me any lover I take would be him. I told him, "yes," just so I could taste his spit. And then he was gone and I was in the woods, running, fully terrified, knowing if I got caught. If I got caught I'd get eaten. Bite by bite and living in pieces in a belly somewhere in Hell. I ran from soundless footsteps, through endless spots of grey and sharp black trees. I ran to a clearing but was blocked by something hanging, caught in the branches that stopped me in my tracks . . . It was hanging in the branches and I couldn't look away. It told me this was inside of me.

This was what summoned him.

When I was awake I talked to him all the time, whenever I got too high or coked out, or too much feeling nothing, too angry and shit, too whatever and I'd do shit like balance on ledges and race on rooftops and tell him he could catch me if I fell to my death. He was my secret. I'd fuck to see how he'd change them, but they never changed. Just stayed boring. For a year nearly, I ran into everything I could, but I couldn't find him. He left. Like I got boring. Just like everybody else. I waited for The Devil, but he wasn't coming. I got so used to walking on this earth being invisible. I was invisible and meaningless. I'd made myself a reflection of a reality made to placate the people I couldn't trust. It was hard to meet their eyes. I'd look at their shadow. At the lies they'd tell.

I became so lonely I began to decipher the black hole in my head. It was instinct; inherited in my DNA and intuition; floated in whispers by my ears from ancestors humming just above my head. My black hole became an ability. It told me things I knew, when I didn't know why I knew them. What they could do, what they meant, how to use them. I continued to live so much like a mirror and so much inside the black hole that it became this world I carried above my shoulders, floating down messages transmitted to me like soft rain from a distant land. All these codes were lit up by light passing through the droplets, just like neurons firing off in the brain. Like stars dying and nebulas vanishing through space-time. Oftentimes in that

long way down as the rain I'd realize some of the
messages might only be for me. Might only be
decipherable in their given form by me. And so,
I kept lots of secrets tucked in parts of me that
would never have to be shaped into sentences. In
parts of me rooted so deep in the ground I forgot
they were mine.

I waited so long I stopped hating myself. Maybe
that was his final test.

I got tired of being so alone. Of knowing things
and being the only one to carry all the messages
in the rain; every day more slipped through my
fingers. One day, I found a way to share my messages. That love hit the ground of my feet like
rain and sprouted seeds that multiplied, dividing
into existences. Into versions of real-life heroes
that people refused to believe in. I'd raise them so
that they could carry what I couldn't, voice what
I didn't have the words for. Acting in place of my
body, I found a way to marry the worlds I lived
in between all my life. I grew with them. I learned
how to look people in the eyes.

I fell in love with what that felt like.

The Devil came back for me one more time. The final time.

He invited me on an adventure of eternal satisfaction. Of never feeling ugly again.

Promising I'd never be heartbroken by loved ones again.

But I no longer needed him.

By then, I'd found my true love.

My true love is being a writer.

Every part of me is human.

Now, I can fight the demons chasing others.

CELINE SONG

Absolutely everyone is invited to my plays. Even my enemies. Even those I do not respect and those I respect too much. Even those who do not speak the language in which my play is written. Sometimes I resent my audience, and sometimes I wish that I had not invited some of them, but still, the invitation extends and extends and extends.

All are welcome. If I can't welcome all, then I would have to admit to my own cowardice, my own worship of capitalism, my own fear of judgment, my own fetishization of safety, my own shaky self-esteem. And it's true—I am scared. I am afraid of an audience that doesn't laugh. I am afraid of an audience that falls asleep. I am afraid of empty seats and unfriendly faces. I am afraid to talk to the audience on their shuffle out of my show. I am afraid of the reviews, the word of mouth, the honest post-show conversations over drinks about my play to which I am never invited.

But I did not become an artist because I am afraid of meeting the world, naked and bare-faced. I am an artist because I love the world, no matter how unfriendly it is to me. I love the world so unconditionally. I want nothing but to be loved back by the world, but I know that it has no obligations to love me back. The only thing I can do is invite the world and dream that I will be understood.

~

My first play, *The Feast*, is about a hostess who invites her friends to a nice dinner party in a world without meat. Her guests are so hungry for meat—so desirous, so desperate—that when her husband finally arrives home, she serves him to them as the main course. This seems to have something to do with how I feel about invitation.

~

In a room where my play is happening, for a period of time—decided by how many words I wrote down on the page for my actors to say—I am the person in charge of the audience's comfort and discomfort. For the ninety minutes or three hours, my audience is locked into a room with my play, and I get to exercise a great deal of power over them. I can put them through traumas, bring up things they do not want to talk about, remind them of something they have long forgotten, give them something to dream about, ask them impossible questions. If I use my power well, I can even make them laugh and cry.

But with great power comes great responsibility. In a room where my play is happening, I am responsible for my audience, just as I am responsible for the friends I have invited to my home.

It is my duty to figure out what they want to drink, what they are hungry for, and where they would like to sit. I have to clearly communicate to them what the rules are. I have to play the right music, light the right scented candles, turn on the right light. I can either have small talk with them or talk about the deep and intimate corners of my soul.

But, just as those I have invited into my home are not allowed into certain spaces (my messy bedroom, for example), the invitation to my work ends at the door into my process. The audience cannot know how I wrote the play. They cannot know the exhausting amount of procrastination.

They cannot know the laziness, the avoidance, the weakness. They cannot know that it took me both so little time and too much time. If they ask, I will have to lie. I will have to make something up.

~

I became a playwright because I am a megalomaniac. As a playwright, I get to write a world into existence. It is a whole world with its own rules, physics, history, ideology, mores, population. It is a world that exists for the ninety minutes or three hours each evening—a world that is created and destroyed over and over again until the run is over.

So what kind of a world do I want to invite my fellow human beings to? The world we live in is cruel. Is the world of my play cruel too? The world we live in is indifferent and amoral. Do I, as the fallible god of my plays, treat my characters with as much indifference and amorality? Children die without meaning in our world. But what about in the world of my play? Does my world punish evil? If so, to what end? If not, why not? Does my world believe in evil at all?

The world of the play usually ends up existing somewhere between a world that gives me pleasure and a world that I think is truthful.

JORDAN TANNAHILL

I invite you to call me any time, day or night, at: +44 7935 637336.

We can talk about art, politics, cute boys. We can call it a performance. Or we could just call it a phone call.

KATE TARKER

Guest List, Arranged Alphabetically

Apollo, anger, anonymity, anecdotes, (some of my)
aunts, breastfeeding, birth, clitoral orgasms, collo-
quialisms, curiosity, children over forty, courage,
confusion, crabbiness, crossed wires,
Dionysus, death, the Enlightenment, the erotic,
error, entertainment, excitement, excess, embar-
rassment, fireworks, formal questions,
gross-out-humor, a grain of salt, the grotesque,
hyperbole, heavy metal, intrigue, insults to intel-
ligence, intuition, illness,
juxtaposition, love,
money money money money,
money money money money,
the middle of the night, mystery,
nudist colonies, nothing human is alien to me (this
is interesting, aka both true and false), outliers,
error, opposites,
obsession, playfulness, punk rock, primal instincts,
pain, pleasure, power,
quickness,

Romanticism, reverse psychology, rest, rigor,
redemption, rage, Republicans???,
satire, surprise, serious subject matter, stillness,
sadness, stupidity, the sublime, subterfuge, seasonal
playwriting (e.g. writing plays set during summer
only when it is summer), spells, skepticism, sensory
overload, error, trust, teenage spirit,
temporary feelings of sanity,
understatement,
vastness, visual art,
victims who are also oppressors, vice versa,
wit,
xxx ratings, yearning, zest

Not Invited

Invitations are for parties. I don't know what theatre is, but it's not a party. Parties have food and
drink, and at the best parties, the food and drink
are free.

Invitations are usually polite. Bla bla bla, the honor
of your company . . .
Invitations are too polite for theatre. I don't know
what theatre is, but it's not polite.

Theatre is a mix of commerce and art. We sell you on our plays. Selling something to you is not an invitation. We make you lust after our unmissable events. Going once. Going twice. Better find your $$$.

But I do curate a guest list. I have to. My theater is full of the Uninvited. It gets crowded, in my head and heart. So, I tip the scales with confetti and plot.

Money gets invited to the theatre. For some reason, it doesn't want to show up on its own.

Theatre is probably a wolf in party clothing.

ALICE TUAN

07.04.18

I invite my demise

Come on
Come along
kill me

try
go on
thrill me

12 creamers from mcdonald's why'd you take em?
every time I eat at mcdonalds I feel like capitalism
wins—

but since you ask:

with one it's a mania
two it's a culture
three a country
four a world
five a universe
six should be galaxies

seven a buncha heaven
eight great
nine fine
ten when
eleven less heaven
twelve by your selve

and mania

without even knowing
(of course
who knowingly invites their demise
wait
there are those
when you do it for the money
or the power
and you don't truly wish to
but society
family
security insists you—
and then
then
that authentic self
that soul
trying to be
best it can

that self
if not numbed
or outsmarted
out-distracted
or out-facted
that self will
yes
invite the demise
of the untrue self)

All I gotta say about that other demise:
karma, Diva

I invited her in
and then she took over
and I was disinvited
from my own home

I invited her in
so I could get kicked out
kicked out of
that
low-grade misery

Yes write me up on those forms
those forms those forms

if only we were talking about shape and sculpture
stead of filling lines on a triplicate

o you're gonna let me go

tolerance you say
just for a change you say

I invite you to my demise
and you let it go
instead of compound it

Well

whatever is next
I'll be sure to invite—

(except you, Diva)

KORDE ARRINGTON TUTTLE

well into the night

one.
writing this high 'cause that's where i am right now.

two.
in my current state of being, well into the night—my boyfriend snoring lightly to my left, a crackling *dew drop, water garden,* and *aegean sea*-scented candle (yes, all three) on the nightstand, to my right—what i'm inviting in is: darkness. it's chaos. fear. with trepidation and humility, i welcome all that seeks to erode what little control i think i have over my life. i welcome what i consciously-and-unconsciously project onto others—in interpersonal exchanges, and through my artistic practices and endeavors. it's time i prioritize deepening my understanding of the whole of me. aspects of my multiplicity that pain me to look at. spend time with. sniff. roll around in my hands. swallow. aspects of my multiplicity that more comfortably belong to *the other*. working to reconcile the world i've inherited with a world

in which *the other* is not relevant. or shouldn't be. there's only *we*. *we* is, of course, wondrously accentuated by the contours of our respective heritages, and cultural makeups. but *we*'s all we got, and *we*'s kidding ourselves to believe otherwise. if i desire to meaningfully contribute to the construction of a collective, life-affirming, culture of belonging (as opposed to individualism), it's imperative that i consciously invite what i pathologically deny, repress, project, and reject into my waking life.

three.
all week, i've wanted to spend time with the ghosts of the early-20th-century west virginia coal miners. wish one would slide into my dm's.

four.
in the back of the lyft, barrelling down 2nd avenue, it becomes immediately clear that this is one invitation i should've considered declining. i accept out of curiosity. i accept because he is powerful. his hands, his spit are everywhere. and, well, so are mine. jingle of his belt buckle. jolt of red lights

turning green. i can't tell if the driver is uncomfortable, or into it. too embarrassed to ask.

five.
some aspects of american history can only be understood though the spirit world. sometimes, the spirit
world opens up to me when i'm high. open-flame,
oil-wick lamp strapped to your heads, you'd descend
deep deep deep into the guts of the mine. every day,
accept the invitation to be consumed by darkness.
not knowing whether or not it'd spit you back out.

MADELINE WISE

One birthday when I was young, I had an Eloise-themed slumber party. I was maybe eight or nine and these were the days before the Internet and Photoshop were things that we all had casual access to, which meant that in order to make the invitations my mom and I painstakingly photocopied pages of the book, then cut out the specific section of each page we wanted to use, then glued those photocopies to one 8.5-by-11 sheet of paper, then wrote the details of my birthday party in my mom's nicest cursive (my own cursive was not up to snuff), and *then* photocopied *that* sheet of paper to make duplicate invitations to be sent out. The party was good, but I don't remember it much. I found one of the invitations in my dad's basement recently and now it's on my fridge. In hindsight the amount of labor it took is sort of astonishing; I feel proud of my past self for being so committed to setting the tone of the party from the jump.

The more I think about it, the more I think that maybe everything is an invitation. I'm a tall woman and for my whole life strangers have interpreted my height as an invitation to comment on my body. (Older short men usually take my height as an invitation to be subtly hostile toward me. It used to upset me and now it delights me.) How I dress and if I do or do not make eye contact with somebody on the subway and what I eat or read in public are all invitations, even when I sometimes don't intend them to be invitations and would prefer that they not be. Laughing at somebody's joke is an invitation as much as the telling of the joke was itself an invitation.

There are fun sexy libidinal invitations that evolve into different more meaningful invitations: with looks, or words, a touch, a joke, your good outfit, your fancy dance moves, you invite someone home from the bar or party; you invite them into your bed and your body; you invite them into some more intimate familiarity with you and your brain; you invite hurt and sorrow but also some sublime expansion of yourself; and then when it's over you invite someone new.

CONTRIBUTORS' BIOS

Will Arbery is a writer for the stage + screen from Texas + Wyoming + seven sisters. His plays include *Plano* (Clubbed Thumb) and *Wheelchair* (3 Hole Press).

Alexander Borinsky is a writer and performer. She recently relocated to Los Angeles, where she is continuing to write and beginning to study permaculture design.

Matty Davis is an artist originally from Pittsburgh, PA, where his grandfather worked for decades in the steel mills and his father's plane crashed. His work seeks physical transformation through effort, play, empathy, geographical journeys, and interpersonal collaboration.

Mashuq Mushtaq Deen is the author of *Draw The Circle* and a New Dramatists resident playwright. He is a fan of the open skies of the American West.

Corinne Donly is a playwright, an educator, and a lover of all things liminal. Their work is about reimagining narrative structure via principles of ecology and play theory.

David Greenspan has worked with many contemporary playwrights, appeared in his own plays and performed solo renditions of dramatic and non-dramatic texts.

Julia Jarcho is a playwright and director from New York City with the company Minor Theater. Her book *Writing and the Modern Stage*: *Theater Beyond Drama* came out in 2017 from Cambridge University Press.

Modesto Flako Jimenez is a Dominican-born, Brooklyn-raised actor, writer, producer, and educator who loves creating DOPE work with DOPE people. www.flakojimenez.com | www.oyegroup.org

Kristine Haruna Lee is a Japanese-Taiwanese-American theater maker, and is co-founder of harunalee theater company. She is the author of *Suicide Forest* (53rd State Press). harunalee.com

Phillip Howze is a playwright living in Brooklyn, NY. His play *Frontieres Sans Frontieres* was produced at The Bushwick Starr and is published by Samuel French.

Mia Katigbak is the founding artistic producing director of NAATCO (National Asian American Theatre Company). She also acts from time to time.

MJ Kaufman is a playwright. With Kit Yan they created a program called Trans Lab that supports emerging trans, nonbinary, and gender noncon-forming artists. Sometimes they also teach or write for TV.

Rachel Marlene Kauder Nalebuff is a writer. She directs 3 Hole Press, a small press for performance works in printed formats.

Sofya Levitsky-Weitz is a playwright, screenwriter, and professor, mostly in Brooklyn but currently in Minneapolis for a Jerome Fellowship at the Play-wrights' Center. She's originally from Los Angeles and mostly dreams of the Pacific Ocean.

Daaimah Mubashshir lives and works in New York City. She writes and performs for Theatre, TV, and Film. www.daaimahmubashshir.com

Caitlin Ryan O'Connell is a freelance director and teaching artist based in New York. She loves collective ideologies, inefficient practices, wandering walks, and tea.

Zach Rufa is a disabled playwright who writes about disability and other things that happen. Also, there's usually magic.

Ren Dara Santiago is a NuYoFilaRican playwright and founding member of Middle Voice at Rattlestick Playwrights Theater. She is a teacher, sister, and artist who believes in multitudes and the supernatural—to varying degrees.

Celine Song is a playwright based in New York. Her play *Endlings* will premiere in 2019 at American Repertory Theater.

Jordan Tannahill is a Canadian playwright, novelist, and director living between London, Budapest, and Toronto.

Kate Tarker is the pen name of American playwright Kate Tarker. She "lives" in Brooklyn.

Alice Tuan is a nationally and internationally

produced playwright and writing facilitator, known for *Ajax (por nobody)*, *Last of the Suns*, *The Roaring Girlie*, *HIT*, and *BATCH: An American Bachelor/ette Party Spectacle*. Before theater, she was an English as a Second Language teacher in Los Angeles and Guangzhou.

Korde Arrington Tuttle is a word-and-image-based-maker from Charlotte, NC. What he makes finds its way into theaters, books, television, and the interwebs.

Madeline Wise is an actor who lives in New York, except when she's elsewhere.

ACKNOWLEDGEMENTS

In the preceding essays, Alexander Borinsky quoted Timothy Morton's *Hyperobjects: Philosophy and Ecology after the End of the World* and George Oppen's *Selected Prose, Daybooks, and Papers*; Kristine Haruna Lee referenced Audre Lorde's 1977 speech, "The Transformation"; Corinne Donly drew on Claudia Rankine's *Don't Let Me Be Lonely: An American Lyric*, Bonnie Marranca's *Ecologies of Theater*, and Gertrude Stein's opus; Zach Rufa tangled with Shakespeare's *Richard III* and Tennessee Williams's *The Glass Menagerie*; and Sofya Levitsky-Weitz cited Aristotle and William Faulkner.

~

We are grateful to Gera Luz for allowing her work to grace our pages and our streets: http://www.geralozano.com/.

~

We are sustained and delighted by our fellow editors and sister presses: Rachel Marlene Kauder

Nalebuff + 3 Hole Press, Matvei Yankelevich + Ugly Duckling Presse, and Tyler Crumrine + Plays Inverse. Together we are fostering an ecosystem for new writing for performance.

Deepest thanks to Karinne Keithley (KK) for starting this press—which illuminated so much for me—and for trusting me (KK) to keep the fire going.

ALSO FROM 53rd STATE PRESS

The Book of the Dog // Karinne Keithley
Joyce Cho Plays // Joyce Cho
No Dice // Nature Theater of Oklahoma
When You Rise Up // Miguel Gutierrez
Montgomery Park, or Opulence // Karinne Keithley
Crime or Emergency // Sibyl Kempson
Off the Hozzle // Rob Erickson
A Map of Virtue + Black Cat Lost // Erin Courtney
Pig Iron: Three Plays // Pig Iron Theatre Company
The Mayor of Baltimore + Anthem // Kristen Kosmas
Ich, Kürbisgeist + The Secret Death of Puppets // Sibyl
Kempson
Soulographie: Our Genocides // Erik Ehn
Life and Times: Episode 1 // Nature Theater of Oklahoma
Life and Times: Episode 2 // Nature Theater of Oklahoma
Life and Times: Episode 3 + 4 // Nature Theater of Oklahoma
The 53rd State Occasional No. 1 // Ed. Paul Lazar
There There // Kristen Kosmas
Seagull (Thinking of you) // Tina Satter
Self Made Man Man Made Land // Ursula Eagly
Another Telepathic Thing // Big Dance Theater
Another Tree Dance // Karinne Keithley Syers
Let Us Now Praise Susan Sontag // Sibyl Kempson
Dance by Letter // Annie-B Parson
Pop Star Series // Neal Medlyn
The Javier Plays // Carlos Murillo
Minor Theater: Three Plays // Julia Jarcho

Ghost Rings (12-inch vinyl) // Half Straddle
A New Practical Guide to Rhetorical Gesture and Action // NTUSA
A Field Guide to iLANDing // iLAND
The 53rd State Occasional No. 2 // Ed. Will Arbery

Forthcoming in 2019

Suicide Forest // Kristine Haruna Lee
Best Behavior // David Levine
A Discourse on Method // David Levine + Shonni Enelow
I Understand Everything Better // David Neumann + Sibyl Kempson
ASTRS // Karinne Keithley
Lipstick Traces // Lana Lesley + the Rude Mechs
Wood Calls Out to Wood // Corinne Donly
Milton // PearlDamour
WATER SPORTS; or insignificant white boys // Jeremy O. Harris

Cover design + photograph by Jonathan Crimmins
Book layout + design by Kate Kremer

53rd State Press publishes lucid, challenging, and lively new writing for performance. Founded in 2007 by Karinne Keithley, it is now managed by Kate Kremer with the support of Laurel Atwell, Tymberly Canale, Anne Cecilia Haney-Demelo, and Antje Oegel. Jess Barbagallo is our brilliant copy-editor.

For more information or to order books, please visit 53rdstatepress.org.

53rd State books are available to the trade through TCG (Theatre Communications Group) and are distributed by Consortium: https://www.cbsd.com.